A Pictorial History of the
CITIES OF SOUTH DAKOTA

ABERDEEN, BROOKINGS, MITCHELL, PIERRE, RAPID CITY, SIOUX FALLS, WATERTOWN & YANKTON

PRESENTED BY THE ARGUS LEADER

This book has been made possible by the

Argus Leader

Table of Contents

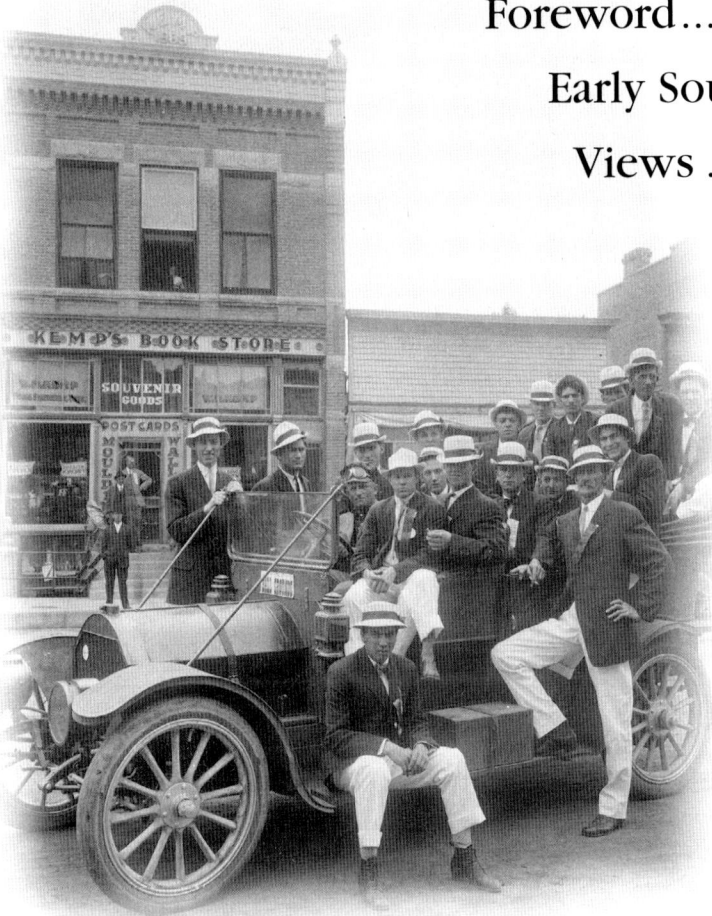

Foreword

The *Argus Leader*, in partnership with the Brookings County History Museum, Codington County Heritage Museum and Historical Society in Watertown, Dacotah Prairie Museum in Aberdeen, Mitchell Area Historical Society, Siouxland Heritage Museums in Sioux Falls, Yankton County Historical Society, and the South Dakota State Historical Society in Pierre, is proud to bring you "A Pictorial History of the Cities of South Dakota."

This book is dedicated to all who have come before us and built the great cities of South Dakota. These are the centers of commerce that define much of what makes South Dakota what it is today.

I hope that as you read about Aberdeen, Brookings, Mitchell, Pierre, Rapid City, Sioux Falls, Watertown and Yankton you will have a greater understanding of their history. Life and culture in and around these communities has shaped much of our state.

The photographs and images seen here date from 1865 to 1938. These images were carefully selected from the extensive collection of local and state archives.

The cities of South Dakota have changed dramatically over the past 140 years. These photographs offer just a glimpse of the changes and the remarkable transition that has made these cities what they are today.

The *Argus Leader* has been an integral part of the South Dakota community almost from the beginning. The first issue of the newspaper was published August 2, 1881. Like the communities featured in this book, the *Argus Leader* has gone through extensive changes over the years, but strives, as in the past, to continue its tradition of bringing the state all the latest in news and information every day.

Thank you to the many people who have worked to make this book a reality, including the museums and historical societies who have shared their photographs and historical knowledge of these cities.

I hope you enjoy this book as much as we have enjoyed putting it together.

Arnold Garson
President and Publisher
Argus Leader

Early South Dakota

Making a go of it has never been a sure thing for South Dakotans.

Long before the Dust Bowl broke their spirit and the Farm Crisis broke their grandchildren's hearts, survival was a daily challenge. Fire, snow and floods changed family fortunes in an instant.

And if not, the next summer offered drought and grasshoppers. Living here has always been about the land and what the land gives back in comfort, beauty, heartache and the fruits of labor.

Communities popped up as little oases with schools, churches, hotels and merchants ready to do business with those who worked the land.

These communities grew with each train, wagon or Model T arriving with someone looking for work or hoping to start a family. The cities were born.

Final rally boosting "Huron for Capital." *Courtesy of Codington County Heritage Museum and Historical Society*

Capitol building, Yankton, on election day, 1866. In the early territorial and statehood period, politics was an all-male activity. Custom forbade the inclusion of women in such election-day gatherings as this one at the legislative hall in Yankton in 1866. Lack of other diversion was partly responsible for the broad interest and involvement in governmental affairs by the rough-clad, generally ill-educated frontiersmen. Men in the community at that time likely to be included in this group were: H.C. Ash, A. Bertlett, D.L. Bramble, Judge Coughton, Nels Colloners, Newton Edmunds, A.W. English, L.H. Eliot, Joseph S. Foster, George S. Foster, Phil Faulk, S.C. Fargo, A.G. Fuller, S.W. Griffith, M.C. Hoyt, _ Hill, _ Hughes, L. Litchfield, Dr. Livingston, M.W. Mathieson, G.C. Moody, S. Morrow, C.P. Myer, George N. Propper, Joseph Prentice, Marc Palmer, _ Reynolds, E.S. Smith, S.L. Spunk, B. N. Smith, _ Smart, J.D. Vanderlinde, Charles Van Epp, G.P. Waldron, and Jim Witherspoon. *Courtesy of Yankton County Historical Society*

The Ash Hotel in Yankton was the scene of much political activity during the legislative sessions at the territorial capital. Innkeeper Henry Ash and his wife provided lodging and meals for lawmakers in the two-story structure built primarily of native cotton-wood lumber. *Courtesy of Yankton County Historical Society*

Steamboats on the Missouri River, circa 1875. The view is at the end of Walnut Street in Yankton. *Courtesy of Yankton County Historical Society*

Downtown scene on a cold winter's day in White, northeast of Brookings. Note the kerosene street lamp on the pole on the lower left. The angle of the sun and the busy street suggest the time as just before Christmas at about 3 p.m. in the afternoon. Perhaps it is shopping for Christmas gifts that has brought everyone out in the cold. *Courtesy of Brookings County History Museum*

Smithsonian Hotel, Yankton, August 7, 1875. *Courtesy of Yankton County Historical Society*

North Broadway in Watertown, 1879. *Courtesy of Codington County Heritage Museum and Historical Society*

The early settlement of Mitchell at Firesteel, 1879. A year after the town was moved to Mitchell, Firesteel was swept away by a flood. The photograph was taken on the business street of Firesteel and shows practically the entire population. The general merchandise store of William Van Eps, one of Firesteel's first settlers, is on the left. *Courtesy of Mitchell Area Historical Society*

Nebraska excursion homesteading near Pierre. *Courtesy of South Dakota State Historical Society*

Central School, Sioux Falls, on the right, was built in 1878. The Norwegian Lutheran Church is on the left. *Courtesy of Siouxland Heritage Museums*

Early streets of Rapid City. *Courtesy of South Dakota State Historical Society*

Elias Thompson and Thomas Thompson were the first settlers north of Medary, Brookings County, 1867. *Courtesy of Brookings County History Museum*

East side of Main Street, Aberdeen, between Third and Fourth avenues, prior to 1888. *Courtesy of Dacotah Prairie Museum*

Pierre stockyards, circa 1885. *Courtesy of South Dakota State Historical Society*

Parrott's mule train in front of Harney Hotel, Rapid City, circa 1890. Mr. Parrott is sitting in the foreground. His mule train is reported to have supplied Gen. Miles who fought at Wounded Knee in 1890. *Courtesy of South Dakota State Historical Society*

Long lines of people waited for the chance to file claims for the lands of the Sisseton Reservation in Watertown, April 15, 1892. *Courtesy of Codington County Heritage Museum and Historical Society*

Morrison Hotel on Third Street in Yankton, 1885. *Courtesy of Yankton County Historical Society*

Coming to Mitchell from Firesteel Valley, circa 1890. *Courtesy of Mitchell Area Historical Society*

The first South Dakota State Capitol building before landscaping, Pierre. *Courtesy of South Dakota State Historical Society*

The first fire-fighting apparatus in Mitchell, circa 1884. *Courtesy of Mitchell Area Historical Society*

Views

The world seems to favor birds, pilots and people with sense enough to look out the windows of tall buildings.

At ground level, South Dakota's cities show the basics of work and play.

But a view from above lets the imagination roam free to consider what life once was and what it could be. Here one sees the ideas of the day — a hotel for guests near the state Capitol, a settlement in the Black Hills, a double-decker bridge across the Missouri.

And here one finds questions with no answer. A panorama in Pierre shows a lone pedestrian on a sidewalk and two more on a bridge. One moment, Watertown streets are lined with cars and people and promise, and in another they are empty. In Aberdeen, a rail yard is underwater.

From above, the eye sees all this. It follows the streets below for blocks and miles, leading to South Dakota's matchless resource, the infinite horizon.

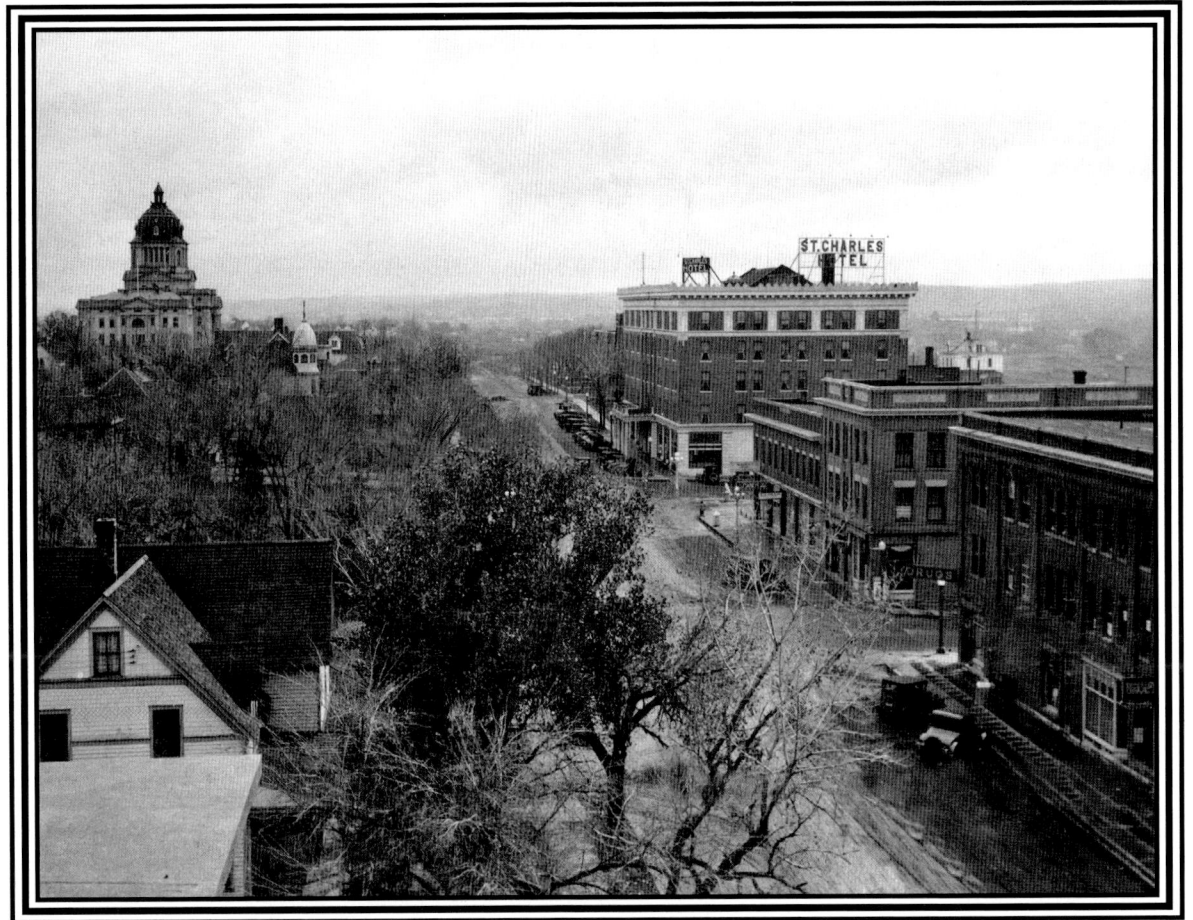

View of Capitol Avenue, Pierre, circa 1925. *Courtesy of South Dakota State Historical Society*

In 1866, seven years after the Indian exodus, Yankton was a treeless village on the Missouri River and seat of government for the vast territory. The largest building, at left, was the Ash Hotel, and directly above it to the east was the original capitol or legislative hall. The dark building slightly to the right was the newly-erected Episcopal Church built by Rev. Melancthon Hoyt, pioneer missionary and chaplain of the Dakota militia. Little evidence of the stockade of 1862 remained. *Courtesy of Yankton County Historical Society*

View of Volga in the early 1900s looking to the north from the Lutheran parsonage building. The first school is in the upper left just beyond an early church. *Courtesy of Brookings County History Museum*

An aerial view of Rapid City, circa 1910. *Courtesy of South Dakota State Historical Society*

Aerial view of Watertown.
Courtesy of Codington County Heritage Museum and Historical Society

Bird's-eye view of Watertown, 1910. *Courtesy of Codington County Heritage Museum and Historical Society*

Aerial view of Pierre, 1911. *Courtesy of South Dakota State Historical Society*

View of Aberdeen looking east from the Milwaukee Railroad freight yard sometime after 1911. *Courtesy of Dacotah Prairie Museum*

Aerial view of Mitchell looking north from Dakota Wesleyan University. *Courtesy of Mitchell Area Historical Society*

The Meridian Highway Bridge, which opened in 1924, crosses the Missouri River at Yankton. The view looks over the Missouri River to Nebraska. *Courtesy of Yankton County Historical Society*

Aerial view of East Watertown, 1928. *Courtesy of Codington County Heritage Museum and Historical Society*

Street Scenes

The street corner was the birthplace of possibilities. Here people did business on a handshake and tipped their hats to a stranger. Boys wearing knickers and neckties compared notes of the day. Men in trench coats measured snow drifts up to their shoulders. The scene was quaint but progressive.

Horses gave way to streetcars. Bicycles made room for automobiles, which men parked diagonally on magnificent miles called Main, Maple and Broadway.

Merchants hung out a shingle or painted a wall to offer dry goods, drugs and OshKosh jeans.

Rain could turn dirt roadways to mud and a blizzard could shut down a town. But when the weather cleared, the street corner kept its place as the pulse of the community.

Crowds gathered downtown Sioux Falls at the intersection of Ninth Street and Phillips Avenue beneath a banner supporting R.F. Pettigrew, circa 1880. *Courtesy of Siouxland Heritage Museums*

Horse-drawn streetcar traveling down a Pierre street, circa 1895. *Courtesy of South Dakota State Historical Society*

Main Avenue of Brookings, circa 1900, looking south and southwest. The First National Bank building is on the right corner. Note the raised sidewalks and unpaved streets. *Courtesy of Brookings County History Museum*

Main Street, Mitchell, circa 1900. *Courtesy of Mitchell Area Historical Society*

Third Street facing east, Yankton, 1903. *Courtesy of Yankton County Historical Society*

Aberdeen street scene, circa 1910. *Courtesy of Dacotah Prairie Museum*

Tents for a special downtown Yankton event can be seen looking east on Third Street from Broadway, 1901. *Courtesy of Yankton County Historical Society*

Looking down the street from in front of Janousek Studio, Yankton. *Courtesy of Yankton County Historical Society*

Phillips Avenue in Sioux Falls under snow, winter of 1909. *Courtesy of Siouxland Heritage Museums*

Chicago & North Western Railroad bridge over Pierre Street in Pierre, circa 1910. *Courtesy of South Dakota State Historical Society*

Business section of Aberdeen, 1912. *Courtesy of Dacotah Prairie Museum*

Looking northeast on Kemp Street and Oak Street North in Watertown.
Courtesy of Codington County Heritage Museum and Historical Society

West side of Pierre Street in Pierre, circa 1910. *Courtesy of South Dakota State Historical Society*

Dakota Avenue, Pierre, circa 1910. First National Bank building is on the corner. *Courtesy of South Dakota State Historical Society*

Third Street facing west in Yankton, February 1915. *Courtesy of Yankton County Historical Society*

Broadway in Watertown, 1930.
Courtesy of Codington County Heritage Museum and Historical Society

Third Street looking east from Broadway in Yankton, circa 1925. The courthouse is in the foreground. *Courtesy of Yankton County Historical Society*

Main Street of Mitchell. A billboard advertises Lon Chaney starring in the movie "Mr. Wu" which premiered in 1927. *Courtesy of Mitchell Area Historical Society*

Billboards on the streets of Pierre, circa 1930. *Courtesy of South Dakota State Historical Society*

Maple Street, Watertown, circa 1935. *Courtesy of Codington County Heritage Museum and Historical Society*

Commerce

A dollar changing hands has great power. Families are fed, whiskers trimmed, brakes greased, shoes shined and cavities filled.

South Dakotans knew this from the start. Making ends meet requires work today on a product or service and then faith tomorrow that someone walks through the door to buy it. It's a principle written on the faces in every town's business district.

Outside the Yankton Steam Laundry, the gentlemen wore vests, the ladies their aprons, children posed smartly to the side and a chestnut steed was ready to deliver the day's work. On Main Street in Mitchell, a sales team prepared to hop into a fleet of cars and speed off through the countryside selling Singer electric sewing machines.

Not everybody succeeded, but those who tried gave South Dakota its reputation as a place where people understand work.

First National Bank, Pierre, circa 1895. *Courtesy of South Dakota State Historical Society*

Widmann Block on South Main Street in Mitchell, circa 1885. *Courtesy of Mitchell Area Historical Society*

B.J. Vann and H. Behrens Furniture and Undertaker at 618 Main Street, Rapid City, circa 1890. *Courtesy of South Dakota State Historical Society*

L. Morris & Company, a dry goods and clothing store, on the corner of Main and Sixth streets, Rapid City, circa 1890. Franklin, Baer & Hall Wholesale Liquor and Cigar Merchants shared the building. *Courtesy of South Dakota State Historical Society*

Merchant's Hotel, Sioux Falls, 1890. *Courtesy of Siouxland Heritage Museums*

Livery and Feed Stable, Rapid City. Gate City Hose Company No. 1 fire wagon is housed in the structure on the left. *Courtesy of South Dakota State Historical Society*

Anton Velig's Bicycle Shop on Broadway in Yankton, 1901. *Courtesy of Yankton County Historical Society*

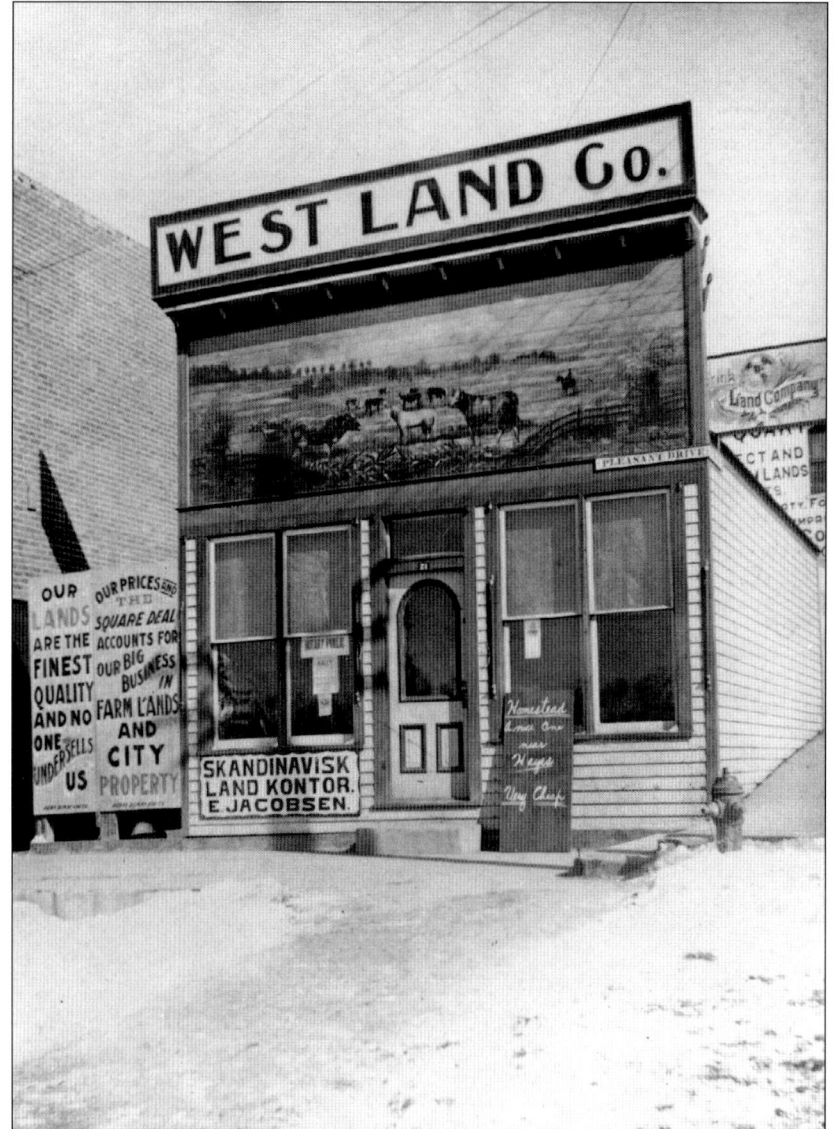

The West Land Co., Pierre. *Courtesy of South Dakota State Historical Society*

Hess and Rau Shop, Watertown, 1896, sold a variety of goods, including bathtubs, indoor toilets, and weather vanes. The man, just to the left of the main doors, has his hand on windmill blades and to his right is a windmill tail vane. *Courtesy of Codington County Heritage Museum and Historical Society*

Inside a Brookings general store at the turn of the century. Included are: Alfred Martinson behind the counter; Lewis Johnson with his pipe; George Nelson; Mrs. Alfred Martinson in back of the lady with the hat; and Julius Martinson holding Alfred Martinson's daughter, Anna. *Courtesy of Brookings County History Museum*

First National Bank of Volga in the early 1900s. *Courtesy of Brookings County History Museum*

First National Bank, Mitchell, circa 1900. *Courtesy of Mitchell Area Historical Society*

Oyloe Studio, a photographer's studio, Brookings, was in operation from 1891 to 1934. *Courtesy of Brookings County History Museum*

Cook's Music Store, Watertown, circa 1905. *Courtesy of Codington County Heritage Museum and Historical Society*

A.S. Peterson Store, Sioux Falls, circa 1915. *Courtesy of Siouxland Heritage Museums*

The Wilcox building in Yankton on the corner of Third and Walnut streets housed American Mortgage, Cramer Law Office, a dentist, and the Yankton Building and Loan Association with E.D. Ward as abstracter. To the right is the post office and the building on the far right is the Yankton Book Bindery. The post office was in this location at 307 Walnut beginning in 1895 for ten years. *Courtesy of Yankton County Historical Society*

Will Pierce, with the moustache, and Nels Arneson inside a Brookings store, circa 1900. *Courtesy of Brookings County History Museum*

Interior of a Yankton drug store around the turn of the century. *Courtesy of Yankton County Historical Society*

The Merchants Bank in Brookings. It was built in 1903 at 314-316 Main Avenue. Post Office employees pictured are: Chas F. Allen, postmaster; Ted Corbin, assistant; Verna Phelps, clerk; Anna Sterns, clerk; and J.W. Kelley, clerk carrier. *Courtesy of Brookings County History Museum*

Howard Hedger Land Office located in the Northwestern Bank building, Aberdeen. Charles A. Howard is fifth from the left.
Courtesy of Dacotah Prairie Museum

Interior of an early Aberdeen business, circa 1905. Essie Zietlow is in the dark dress and W.F. Langc, bookkeeper, is standing. *Courtesy of Dacotah Prairie Museum*

Cataract Hotel burned in 1900 and was rebuilt in 1901 at the corner of Ninth Street and Phillips Avenue. *Courtesy of Siouxland Heritage Museums*

Yankton Steam Laundry with their delivery truck in front, 307 West 3rd Street, Yankton. *Courtesy of Yankton County Historical Society*

W.H. Wilson funeral home, 508 South Main, Aberdeen, 1905. *Courtesy of Dacotah Prairie Museum*

Herb Pike Store, 308 West Third Street, Yankton. *Courtesy of Yankton County Historical Society*

Edgerton and Coacher Livery Barn, 318 Douglas Street, Yankton, 1904. *Courtesy of Yankton County Historical Society*

C.A. McArthur Farm Machinery store at Third Avenue East and Lincoln Street, Aberdeen, circa 1905. *Courtesy of Dacotah Prairie Museum*

Loonan Lumber Company, Sioux Falls, circa 1905. *Courtesy of Siouxland Heritage Museums*

Dreamland Theater was the first movie theater in Rapid City, 1909. *Courtesy of South Dakota State Historical Society*

Cars loaded and "Bound for Canada" for the Luse Land & Development Co., Aberdeen, 1909. *Courtesy of Dacotah Prairie Museum*

Granite Block, Watertown, circa 1910. South Dakota architect W.L. Dow designed the building constructed in 1887. Businesses located there included: the Lund Land Company, Northwestern Life Insurance Company, and several doctors' offices. *Courtesy of Codington County Heritage Museum and Historical Society*

Will A. Beach Printing Company, Sioux Falls, circa 1910. *Courtesy of Siouxland Heritage Museums*

Inside Excelsior Autocycles, Mitchell, circa 1913. *Courtesy of Mitchell Area Historical Society*

J.F. Anderson Lumber Company office was located in the 700 block on North Main Street, Mitchell, 1914. Carl West was the manager; Ed Moore is the second man. *Courtesy of Mitchell Area Historical Society*

Cigar store operated by Carl. O. Swanson in the lobby of Citizens Bank, Aberdeen, circa 1915. *Courtesy of Dacotah Prairie Museum*

Interior of the Fisher Hardware Store, Pierre, circa 1915. *Courtesy of South Dakota State Historical Society*

Ben Boussell's men's clothing store, Aberdeen, 1915. *Courtesy of Dacotah Prairie Museum*

The Sugar Bowl restaurant, Sioux Falls, circa 1918. *Courtesy of Siouxland Heritage Museums*

Interior of Johnson Furniture Store at its second location in Mitchell on the west side of Main Street, circa 1916. *Courtesy of Mitchell Area Historical Society*

Rivola Barber Shop, 206 West Third Street, Yankton. Joe Rivola is in the foreground; Roy Walving is in the center. *Courtesy of Yankton County Historical Society*

Harry C. Nelsen Auto Garage, Yankton, circa 1915. *Courtesy of Yankton County Historical Society*

Employees of Thompson Yards, Inc., with a truckload of lumber, 1919, Aberdeen. *Courtesy of Dacotah Prairie Museum*

Fantles Department Store, Sioux Falls, 1918. The store was at 117 South Phillips Avenue until 1938 when it moved to Ninth Street and Main Avenue.

Courtesy of Siouxland Heritage Museums

A truckload of hay in front of Western Automotive Company at Main and Railroad streets in Mitchell, circa 1920. *Courtesy of Mitchell Area Historical Society*

Brookings Farmers Co-op, May 1919. *Courtesy of Brookings County History Museum*

The 1918 crop of Cossack alfalfa seed in front of the Pierre depot. The load was valued at $3,755. *Courtesy of South Dakota State Historical Society*

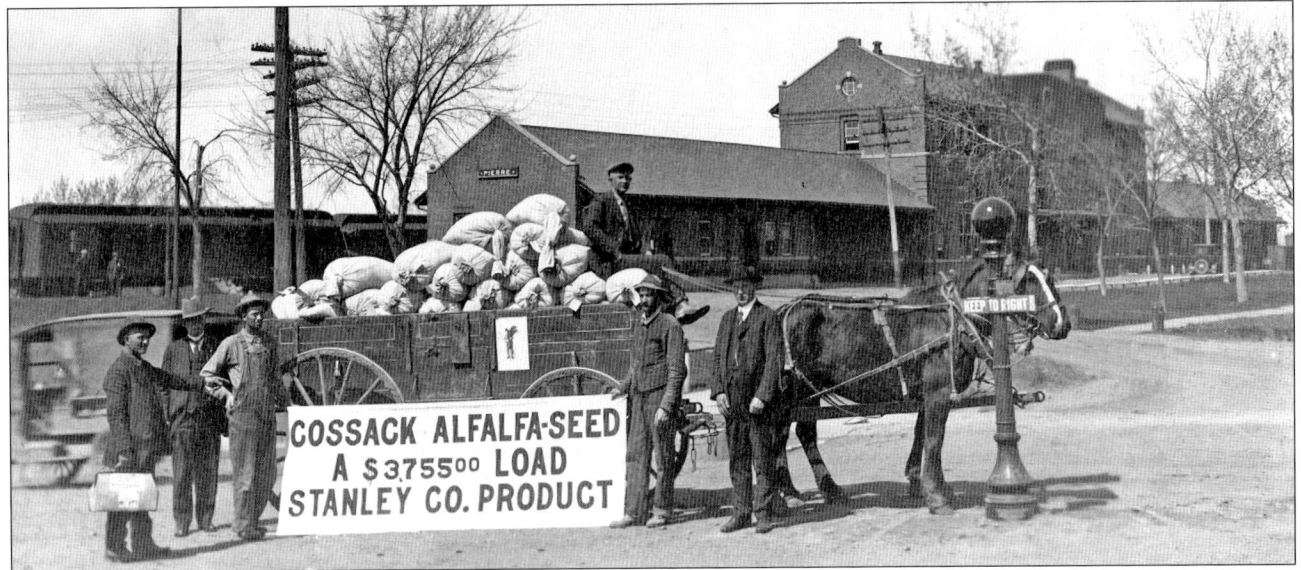

COSSACK ALFALFA-SEED
A $3,755.00 LOAD
STANLEY CO. PRODUCT

Ed N. Olson grocery store in Aberdeen, 1923. Their business was boosted by the close proximity of the Rebekah and Odd Fellows Lodge. *Courtesy of Dacotah Prairie Museum*

J.C. Penney Company building, Mitchell, 1926. The building started out as the Western Bank building. *Courtesy of Mitchell Area Historical Society*

Yankton Brake Service, A.R. Bade, Proprietor. *Courtesy of Yankton County Historical Society*

Nelson and Reed Hardware, Watertown, circa 1925. *Courtesy of Codington County Heritage Museum and Historical Society*

Palm Gardens. a popular restaurant and bar in Aberdeen, circa 1925. *Courtesy of Dacotah Prairie Museum*

Singer Company salespeople and employees posed next to cars in front of the Allerson-Millinery store which sold Singer sewing machines, 406 North Main Street, Mitchell, 1928. The Red Owl Grocery is next door and Coxe Printing is on the far right. *Courtesy of Mitchell Area Historical Society*

Conklin Drug Store, Pierre. *Courtesy of South Dakota State Historical Society*

Interior of The Lighthouse electrical store, formerly Addison Electric, in Watertown, 1927. Pictured are: Jesse Christianson, electrician; Loren Antritter; and Chas D. Antritter, owner. The Irish water spaniel "Bum" made a dive for the photographer when the flash went off. *Courtesy of Codington County Heritage Museum and Historical Society*

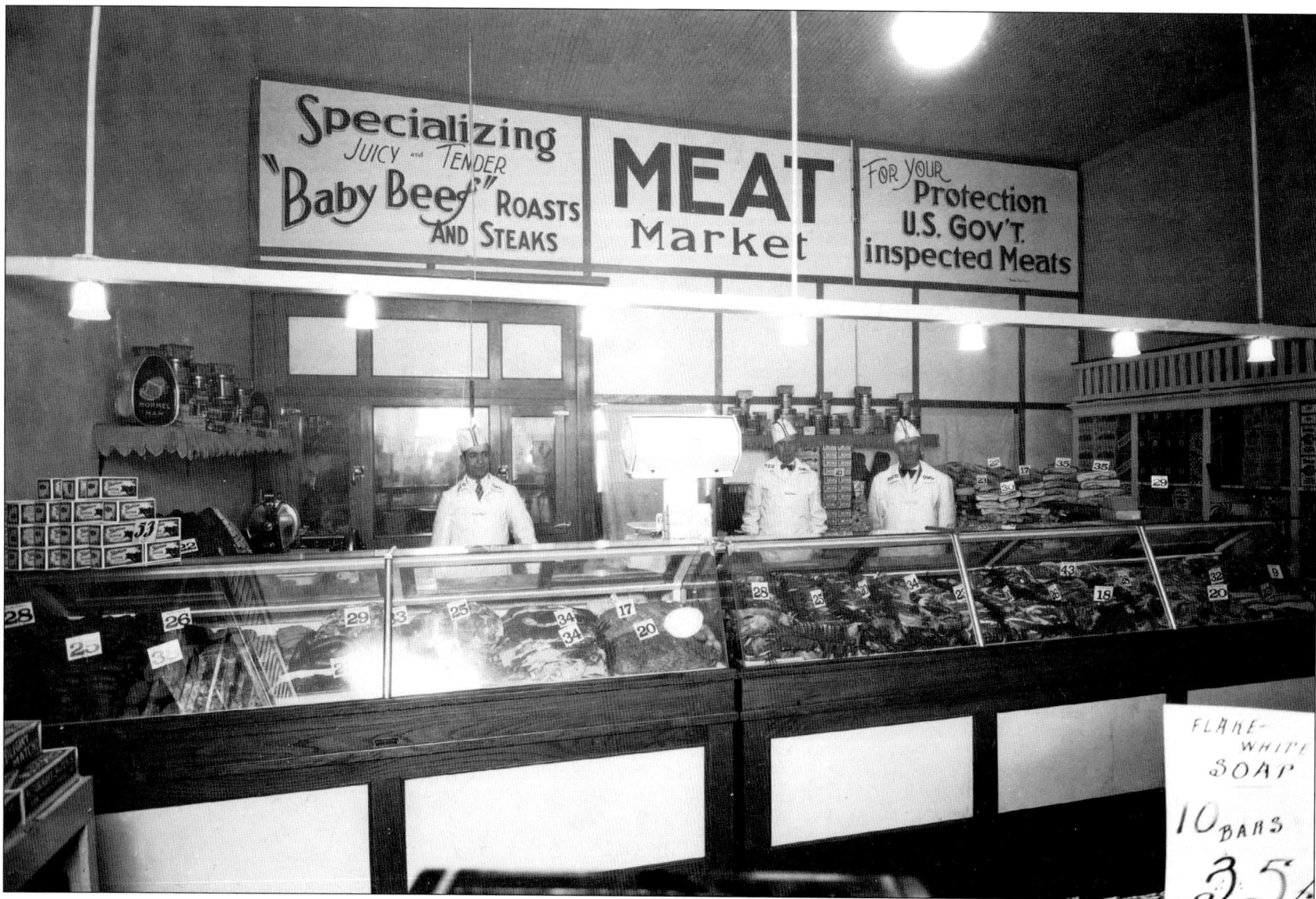

Meat Market, Pierre, April 1929. *Courtesy of South Dakota State Historical Society*

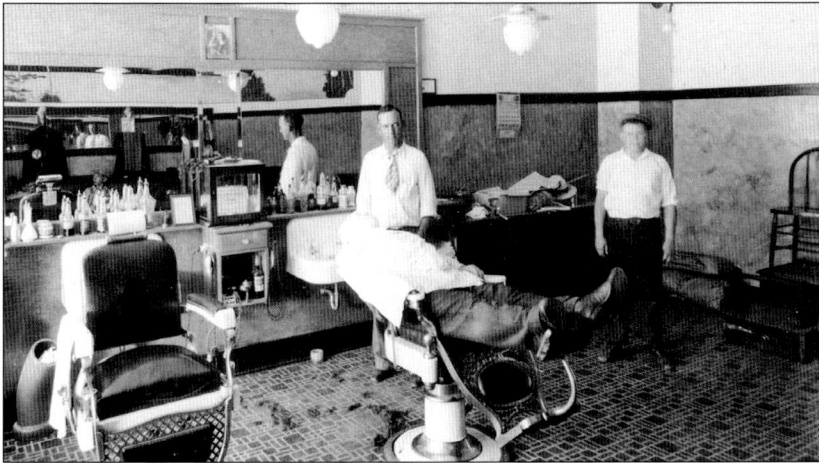

Woodard's barber shop, Volga, July 1929. James Wright is in the chair, George Woodard is the barber, and Louis Scanlan is available to apply the boot black. *Courtesy of Brookings County History Museum*

A radio flown in for Miller Studio in Pierre, August 18, 1929. Guy Bulow is in the pinstripe suit. *Courtesy of South Dakota State Historical Society*

Hotel Lincoln, Watertown. *Courtesy of Codington County Heritage Museum and Historical Society*

Peoples Market and delivery truck in Pierre, circa 1930. *Courtesy of South Dakota State Historical Society*

Johnson Furniture Store and Staehle Hardware Co., 3rd Avenue and Lawler Street, Mitchell, 1930. Viking Oldsmobile is on the far left and a White Eagle service station is in the foreground on the right. *Courtesy of Mitchell Area Historical Society*

WNAX Fair Price Station, 114 Douglas Avenue, Yankton. In the 1930s and 1940s, Yankton radio station WNAX became a driving force behind economic and social issues. In protest to the high gasoline prices during the Great Depression, the Gurneys opened the WNAX Fair Price station in Yankton, selling gas four cents cheaper than the going rate. The station also pioneered the raising of drought and disaster relief funds and handed out free maps during World War II. *Courtesy of Yankton County Historical Society*

Economy Grocery, Pierre, circa 1935. You could buy five dozen oranges for 85 cents. *Courtesy of South Dakota State Historical Society*

Carlsen's Drive In on West Sixth Street in Brookings. *Courtesy of Brookings County History Museum*

Dakota Tavern, Sioux Falls. *Courtesy of Siouxland Heritage Museums*

Odemark's Bar, 1938, Pierre. The business opened in 1891 and featured a hand-carved black walnut bar. *Courtesy of South Dakota State Historical Society*

Industry

Industries in South Dakota's cities have worked to meet each other's interlocking needs.

Some of the work has been hot and dirty, some of it not for the squeamish. But it all shows what can happen when enterprising people rally around an idea.

Horse-drawn ice wagons rattled through Sioux Falls. Well diggers continued an ancient craft. Biscuit workers and meat cutters answered the bell each morning. A businessman from Wisconsin wishing to open an iron and boiler works built his plant in Mitchell with wood hauled by ox cart from Yankton.

The efforts have never been quite able to match the opportunities because of a simple equation. South Dakota is long on space and short on people.

But as labor-saving devices spread through the economy, industrial output increased.

The Sioux Falls John Morrell plant from Penitentiary Hill, August 1930. *Courtesy of Siouxland Heritage Museums*

The Mitchell brick yards were one and one-half miles from the city. They provided bricks for much of the city's early buildings including the Hitchcock Block, Bourne Block, and Letcher Block.
Courtesy of Mitchell Area Historical Society

First kiln in Rapid City. *Courtesy of South Dakota State Historical Society*

Volga Mill, circa 1900. *Courtesy of Brookings County History Museum*

Queen Bee Mill and falls at Sioux Falls, 1895. The mill, which used the power of the falls to grind wheat into flour, was adversely affected by drought years as in this 1895 photograph with low water and no crops. *Courtesy of Siouxland Heritage Museums*

John Condon in Bernt Christiansen's harness shop in the early 1900s, Yankton. *Courtesy of Yankton County Historical Society*

Well diggers with their equipment, Brookings. The Skinner building, built in 1901, is in the background. Brookings House burned in 1910. *Courtesy of Brookings County History Museum*

George H. Summers, right, founder of Mitchell Iron and Supply Co., with two unidentified men and his son, Frank, on the left, repairing an Avery steam tractor at their machine shop. *Courtesy of Mitchell Area Historical Society*

Mitchell Iron and Supply Company, 217 West First Street, was founded in 1884 by George S. Summers as the Mitchell Iron and Boiler Works. Summers came to Mitchell from Wisconsin after the Civil War. He constructed the building with lumber hauled by ox cart from Yankton. The business started as a machine shop, foundry, boiler works, and farm machinery repair business. *Courtesy of Mitchell Area Historical Society*

Employees of the John Morrell Company construction department under Supt. G.W. RuDesill, Sioux Falls, 1911. *Courtesy of Siouxland Heritage Museums*

Manchester Biscuit Company employees, Sioux Falls, circa 1911, from left to right: Bert Fish, Henry Nelson, Charlie Christ, Elmer Nelson, Rollo Pratt, unknown, "Gloomy" Gus Eckholm, John Harmeur, Carl Entenmen, unknown, Walter Robinson, Josephine Lind, Hannah Larson, Lillian Elmen, Sadie Pederson, Marie Voit, Ruth Sattre, Clara Bradley, Clara Hagan, Datta Dawse, Martha Peterson, Alice Martin, Veronica Cox, Ralph Holland, Dick Vanderberg, Gladys Merritt, Irene Bresee, Agnes Cox, Norma Griffin, and "Spike" Earl Inseth. *Courtesy of Siouxland Heritage Museums*

Print shop in the Public Opinion Building, in Watertown, circa 1918. Mr. D.E. Café is seated in the front, Elrah Leftgard is behind him, and Clarence Halvorson is standing. *Courtesy of Codington County Heritage Museum and Historical Society*

Mullen-Rourke Ice Company, Sioux Falls, circa 1925. *Courtesy of Siouxland Heritage Museums*

An early-day Brookings roller flour mill next to the Chicago North Western Railroad track at the south end of Brookings' Main Street. *Courtesy of Brookings County History Museum*

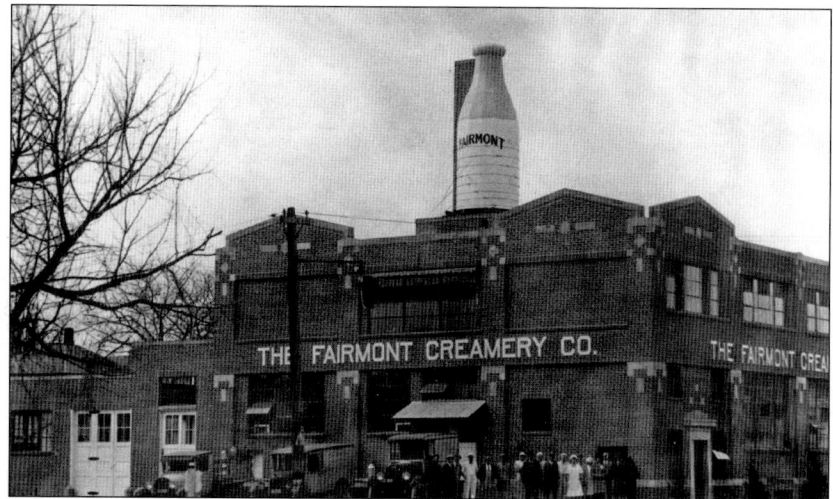

Fairmont Creamery Company, Rapid City, circa 1925. *Courtesy of South Dakota State Historical Society*

Gurney Seed & Nursery Co., Yankton, 1924. *Courtesy of Yankton County Historical Society*

Newsroom at the Argus Leader, Sioux Falls, January 1930. *Courtesy of Siouxland Heritage Museums*

Armour Creameries, Mitchell, 1929. *Courtesy of Mitchell Area Historical Society*

Meat packing plant, beef kill taken January 7, 1937, in Rapid City. *Courtesy of South Dakota State Historical Society*

Transportation

Getting from here to there in South Dakota is an errand of patience.

A drive from Elk Point to Ladner would take 10 hours and a coffee break. An evening trip across the Missouri at Platte requires an eye for deer on the highway.

South Dakotans have propelled themselves a number of ways. Steamboats, ferries, barges and kayaks have cut through the Missouri. A two-story bridge spanned the river at Yankton. Horses pulled carriages across a pontoon bridge in Pierre.

With the rise of the automobile, a Sioux Falls creation called the Fawick Flyer became a picture of elegance with gentlemen in derbies cavorting about at speeds of 60 miles an hour.

Sleighs and passenger trains had their day. An electric streetcar once carried passengers from the state's biggest city to a now-forgotten quarry town called East Sioux Falls.

When people had to get somewhere, they found a way.

The *B.A. Douglass* goes under the lifted span of the newly-built Meridian Bridge over the Missouri River, Yankton, July 30, 1924. Note the onlookers on the bridge. *Courtesy of Yankton County Historical Society*

Sidney stage by Florman Block on St. Joe and Sixth streets, Rapid City, 1880. *Courtesy of South Dakota State Historical Society*

Ferry boat on the Missouri River, circa 1880. *Courtesy of Yankton County Historical Society*

Horse-drawn funeral hearses, Pierre, circa 1890. *Courtesy of South Dakota State Historical Society*

Clews Brothers Dray Line, Brookings, circa 1900. *Courtesy of Brookings County History Museum*

Joe Daum, Jr., in his horse-drawn buggy early in the 1900s in Brookings County. *Courtesy of Brookings County History Museum*

Chicago & North Western depot at Pierre, 1909. *Courtesy of South Dakota State Historical Society*

Pontoon bridge at Coteau Street, Pierre, circa 1900. *Courtesy of South Dakota State Historical Society*

Moving a tree past the Press building at the corner of 4th and Walnut streets in Yankton, circa 1900. The Press and Daily Dakotan was on the first floor of the building and the Elks Club is in the upstairs. William M. Wallner is the man on the front of the sled with the white collar. *Courtesy of Yankton County Historical Society*

Winter scene on Walnut and Second streets in Yankton, circa 1905. *Courtesy of Yankton County Historical Society*

Fawick Flyer, 1910. This car was built at Sioux Falls by N.O. and Thomas L. Fawick in the winter and spring of 1909-10 at 821 West Thirteenth Street. N.O. Fawick is at the wheel, Thomas L. Fawick in the back seat, and Oswald T. Klypp in the front seat. Thomas Fawick was born in 1889 in Sioux Falls and at the age of seventeen went into business for himself designing and building cars. The Fawick Flyers were some of the first to have four doors and could go sixty miles an hour. They were said to be "quiet" cars, even though they could be heard four blocks away. When his cars did not sell well, Fawick left Sioux Falls to work for a company in Wisconsin. *Courtesy of Siouxland Heritage Museums*

"From Brookings to Los Angeles" in front of First National Bank in Brookings, circa 1910. Jim Natesta and Hal Morehouse are in the Buick automobile and are about to leave for Los Angeles. This was the first Buick to make an overland trip to California and back from Brookings. The owner and driver was James Natesta, an early merchant of Medary and Brookings, and his companion, H.C. Morehouse. *Courtesy of Brookings County History Museum*

Streetcars in front of the Pierre Savings Bank, which later became the First National Bank, circa 1900. *Courtesy of South Dakota State Historical Society*

Electric streetcar on the South Dakota Rapid Transit and Railroad Co., the only interurban railroad in the state, circa 1910. *Courtesy of Siouxland Heritage Museums*

Sioux Falls traction system on the corner of Fourteenth Street and Summit Avenue, circa 1910. *Courtesy of Siouxland Heritage Museums*

Waiting at the Bruce depot, circa 1910, including Lloyd Ribstein, Ray Pickering, and Andrew Eklund. *Courtesy of Brookings County History Museum*

Chicago & North Western depot, Watertown. *Courtesy of Codington County Heritage Museum and Historical Society*

Chicago, Rock Island & Pacific-Minneapolis & St. Louis (CRI&P-M&St.L) depot at Watertown. *Courtesy of Codington County Heritage Museum and Historical Society*

Milk shipment at the Aberdeen depot on the Chicago, Milwaukee & St. Paul Railroad. *Courtesy of Dacotah Prairie Museum*

Chicago and North Western depot at Aberdeen shortly after it was built in 1910. The canopy was 250 feet long and sheltered the block-long platform for waiting passengers. *Courtesy of Dacotah Prairie Museum*

Yankton Pathfinders of Meridian Road starting out, circa 1915. *Courtesy of Yankton County Historical Society*

Airplane hanger built in west Watertown in 1919 by Walter L. Cooke. On the left is Walter's son, Lavonne, a pilot who started the Watertown School of Flying that same year. *Courtesy of Codington County Heritage Museum and Historical Society*

Ferry taking a car across the river at Pierre, circa 1920. *Courtesy of South Dakota State Historical Society*

Vehicle crossing the wooden pontoon bridge over the Missouri River at Yankton, circa 1920. *Courtesy of Yankton County Historical Society*

View from the east of the bridge over the Missouri River, Yankton, 1924. *Courtesy of Yankton County Historical Society*

Building the car bridge at Pierre over the Missouri River, February 20, 1926. *Courtesy of South Dakota State Historical Society*

Skyline Drive, Rapid City. Stein Banks was the engineer designer on this W.P.A. project, circa 1935. *Courtesy of South Dakota State Historical Society*

Silvertown Days at Soo Skyways. Soo Skyways near Forty-first Street and Western Avenue, was an early airport in Sioux Falls in the 1930s. Goodrich tires were popular airplane tires, especially after Charles Lindbergh's trans-Atlantic flight in 1927. *Courtesy of Siouxland Heritage Museums*

Public Service

Public service generally is no way to become wealthy, and some of the work is thankless. Why else would elections, even for Legislature, run short on candidates?

But in emergencies and the humdrum of daily living, South Dakota has been democracy on display, with everyday citizens taking responsibility for the general welfare. There's a loneliness to this, as a rural school teacher would attest, and a respect that captures the public attention. It showed when Civil War veterans reunited on a wooden sidewalk and when World War I draftees swarmed a train depot.

Public service is as basic as neighbors working together in fire departments. But South Dakotans never have lost sight of the moment when the leader of the free world visits. Theodore Roosevelt spoke forcefully in Yankton. Calvin Coolidge appeared more reserved posing with a brass band in Rapid City. Each scene shows free people at work.

Charles Pickett's grading crew on the grounds of the newly-completed capitol building in Pierre, 1910.
Courtesy of South Dakota State Historical Society

Post of G.A.R. and the Women's Relief Corps, Watertown, circa 1895. *Courtesy of Codington County Heritage Museum and Historical Society*

The Dakota Hospital for the Insane, circa 1890. The hospital was opened in 1879 in a frame building constructed from pieces of two other buildings. It housed patients, employees, a kitchen, dining room, laundry, and everything else. A new brick building to replace it was built in 1881. It was almost finished in December when the wooden structure burned to the ground in 30 minutes, resulting in the deaths of five patients. No equipment could be salvaged. *Courtesy of Yankton County Historical Society*

Minnehaha County Courthouse, Sioux Falls, before the clock was added to the tower in 1892. *Courtesy of Siouxland Heritage Museums*

Courthouse at Pierre, 1900. *Courtesy of South Dakota State Historical Society*

The Mitchell Fire Department, displaying their championship banner and fire-fighting equipment, circa 1895. *Courtesy of Mitchell Area Historical Society*

Troops of the First South Dakota Volunteer Infantry were rushed into federal service following the declaration of war on Spain in April of 1898. Various companies were assembled in Sioux Falls and ultimately shipped to the Philippine Islands where they fought Filipino insurrectionists rather than Spaniards. *Courtesy of Yankton County Historical Society*

The Watertown Fire Department, 1903. Top row, from left to right: Pete Peterson, Chas E. Brickell, Carl Promhouse, Chas Hamilton, Frank Melton, H.C. Chrisnacht, Paul Laqua, Jerry Watkins, and Frank Marston. Second row: George Anderson, Don Livingston, Frank Bennet, Frank Bramble, Clem Govers, Tom Devyer, Charles Lyon, Matt Middelton, Sam Welch, Walt McLaughlin, John Scott, and William Minard. Third row: Chief Arnold Reichert, William Luck, William McLaughlin, Robert Baldwin, George T. Hipp, James Jensen, Irvin McLaughlin, Jim Skinner, Lou Ohler, J.A. Timmerman, Martin Belatti, and Frank Munger. Bottom row: Henry Christopherson, Frank Scott, Peter Powderly, Fred McLaughlin, dog, Steve Skinner, Joe Devyer, and Frank Elkins.

Courtesy of Codington County Heritage Museum and Historical Society

Hughes County Courthouse, Pierre. The tower was later removed. *Courtesy of South Dakota State Historical Society*

U.S. President Teddy Roosevelt in Yankton, 1903. *Courtesy of Yankton County Historical Society*

The State Penitentiary at Sioux Falls was built in 1882. Richard F. Pettigrew, territorial delegate to Congress, had secured funding to build the prison in 1881. This photo, taken in 1906, shows the tower, cell block, and warden's residence. *Courtesy of Siouxland Heritage Museums*

Laying the cornerstone for South Dakota's State Capitol, Pierre, June 25, 1908. *Courtesy of South Dakota State Historical Society*

Men hauling pillars for the new capitol, Pierre, circa 1909. The old wooden capitol is on the left. *Courtesy of South Dakota State Historical Society*

Back of the Watertown Post Office from the southeast corner, 1909. *Courtesy of Codington County Heritage Museum and Historical Society*

Carnegie Library, Pierre, 1909. *Courtesy of South Dakota State Historical Society*

Yankton Courthouse and County Jail, circa 1910. *Courtesy of Yankton County Historical Society*

Codington County Courthouse, Watertown, 1911. *Courtesy of Codington County Heritage Museum and Historical Society*

Brown County Courthouse, Aberdeen, 1912. *Courtesy of Dacotah Prairie Museum*

Brookings County Courthouse, circa 1915. *Courtesy of Brookings County History Museum*

World War I draftees leaving from the depot in Brookings, circa 1918. *Courtesy of Brookings County History Museum*

U.S. President Calvin Coolidge and Peck's Band, circa 1925. Bill Peck, the band director and a musician of regional repute, is standing to the left of President Coolidge. Peck was invited to bring his band to Rapid City to entertain the President during his visit to the Black Hills in the 1920s. The photo is probably at the Rapid City High School that was the "Western White House" for Coolidge's visit. *Courtesy of Codington County Heritage Museum and Historical Society*

The Watertown Fire Department, circa 1925. *Courtesy of Codington County Heritage Museum and Historical Society*

Education

Yesterday's snapshots show two things about education in South Dakota.

One is that 100 years ago students spent a fair amount of time to look nice. It's unlikely today that students dress in black for poultry class in Brookings or in white ruffles for the class photo in Watertown.

The other is that education, as much as any other function of a free society, illustrates the power of people connecting to people.

The eyes on each face represent a mind that someone thought was important. It began at home. It continued at school. It's the same for the boys in uniform at the Pierre Indian School as for the man in the suit with hand on hip at the back of the class in Aberdeen.

They're all gone now. But the connection lives on, one mind to the next, a water bucket filled with facts for survival and prosperity, an open field for creative expression.

Students and teachers of Washington School, Pierre, November 17, 1902. *Courtesy of South Dakota State Historical Society*

Washington School, Pierre, 1895. *Courtesy of South Dakota State Historical Society*

Dakota Hall at Sixth and Walnut streets, Yankton, circa 1880. *Courtesy of Yankton County Historical Society*

Crowd gathered at Century Memorial Hall at Dakota Wesleyan University in Mitchell, circa 1880. It later became known as Graham Hall. *Courtesy of Mitchell Area Historical Society*

Lincoln School, Sioux Falls, was designed in 1888 by local architect Wallace Dow. The school was torn down in 1915. *Courtesy of Siouxland Heritage Museums*

Brookings High School, known as the Red Castle, was built in August 1888 and cost $10,000. In 1935, it was torn down and a new building was built for junior high students at a cost of $90,000. *Courtesy of Brookings County History Museum*

Brookings County School District #58, 1898. Sitting, left to right: Bessy Ladd, Ottilie Beck, Oscar Beck, and Henry _. Second row: Carl Schultz, Bennie Friedel, Ansel Kerr, Adolph Schultz with Tom Kerr peeking over his head, Ed Kerr, Otto Schwenke, Henry Schwenke, Leonard Ladd, Mary Kerr, Agnes Beck, and Amanda Friedel. Top row: August Schwenke, Sherman Ladd, John Ladd, Agnes Kerr, Henry Schultz, Agnes Schwenke, and teacher Ida Fiedel. *Courtesy of Brookings County History Museum*

Students at Daum School, circa 1900, include: Johnnie Smal, Bert Krum, Lillian Schwartz, Myrtle Krumm, Ethel Krumm, three Idsmore children, Emma Sorenson, Annie Erickson, Jennie Small, and George Erickson.

Courtesy of Brookings County History Museum

Jefferson School, Aberdeen, was built in 1891. *Courtesy of Dacotah Prairie Museum*

Poultry class at South Dakota State College in Brookings, 1902. *Courtesy of Brookings County History Museum*

State School of Mines, Rapid City. *Courtesy of South Dakota State Historical Society*

Seth Gilborne and Isaac Lincoln inspecting the new well at Northern Normal and Industrial School, Aberdeen, 1902. *Courtesy of Dacotah Prairie Museum*

Watertown High School class of 1902. Rolla Williams is sitting front and center. *Courtesy of Codington County Heritage Museum and Historical Society*

Aberdeen classroom, March 5, 1915. *Courtesy of Dacotah Prairie Museum*

Scene on the South Dakota State College grounds in Brookings. *Courtesy of Brookings County History Museum*

All Saints School, Sioux Falls, opened September 1885. The building was built of quartzite and was designed by Wallace Dow. *Courtesy of Siouxland Heritage Museums*

Rapid City Grade and High School after the bell tower was removed, 1912. *Courtesy of South Dakota State Historical Society*

Yankton High School, June 5, 1914. Front row, left to right: Olive Dilger, Adolph Pederson, Lucile Wright, Agnes Brennan, Oliver Norton, Mae Swinhoe, and Ira Pease. Second row: Ruth Summers, Frank Rogers, Catherine Walsh, Art Rogers, Betty Bates, Jim Donahue, Bessie Burgi, and Bill Dunn. Third row: Tart Bowers, C. Gurney, Ray Milliken, Edith Ford, Bill Kositzky, Bill Bolwat, Lillie Krenkle, Roy Milliken, Amelia Bolnowsky, and Kent Hartung. *Courtesy of Yankton County Historical Society*

South Dakota State College students on the steps of the extension building, circa 1915. *Courtesy of Brookings County History Museum*

Pierre High School, 1911. *Courtesy of South Dakota State Historical Society*

Aberdeen High School shortly after it was built, 1911. *Courtesy of Dacotah Prairie Museum*

Fifth grade students from Irving School, Sioux Falls, circa 1915. Irving School was the first public school building in Sioux Falls and was built in 1873. *Courtesy of Siouxland Heritage Museums*

Students at the Pierre Indian School. *Courtesy of South Dakota State Historical Society*

Eighth grade graduating class, Watertown, circa 1916. *Courtesy of Codington County Heritage Museum and Historical Society*

South Side School in Mitchell was built in 1894 and replaced in 1920.
Courtesy of Mitchell Area Historical Society

Mitchell Junior High School was built in 1920 at 3rd Avenue and Sanborn
Street. *Courtesy of Mitchell Area Historical Society*

Looking toward the Main Building at Dakota Wesleyan University at
Mitchell, 1925. *Courtesy of Mitchell Area Historical Society*

Yankton High School students, circa 1925. *Courtesy of Yankton County Historical Society*

Mitchell High School, class of 1926. Front row, left to right: Sid Anderson, Everett Kanouff, Perry Paullin, Dayle Gunter, Harlan Peterson, Mervin Wheeler, Gordon Patterson, Bob Curtis, advisor Glen Stanley, Harvard Noble, and William Fritz, Jr. Second row: Cathryn Ahern, Evelyn Moore, Luella Hughes, Ruth Forrest, Mary Johnston, Edith Ellingson, Gert Schumway, Esther Heather, Odessa Conrad, Kathryn Larrison, Helen Corcoran, Charlotte Leighty, Harriet Redline, Grace Richards, Evelyn Wipf, unknown, Vera Halsted, and Howard Giese. Third row: Geneva Tucker, unknown, Marie Berg, unknown, Lucille Baillie, Edith Richards, Ernestine Zollman, advisor Ruth Ann Condon, advisor Grace Laxon, Freda Pusch, Alice Welch, Irene Mathieson, unknown, Florence Bates, Herbert Wilcox, and Elmer Ollenburg. Fourth row: Daphne Kennedy, unknown, Martha Gruenwald, Evelyn Wipf, Gladys Foss, Margaret Scott in the rear, hidden person is unknown, Hazel Smith, Hallie Kimple, Loula Avery, Margurite Mather next to the lamp post, unknown, and Edgar Henzlik. *Courtesy of Mitchell Area Historical Society*

Sports & Leisure

They couldn't be happier. The guys in their suits and the gals in their dresses, seated properly on the rocks, are fishing for bullheads in the Sioux River.

South Dakotans know how to work and how to play.

Play has been formal, or else the Methodists might not have dressed up for their boat ride in 1915.

And it's been informal. Skinny dippers in Mitchell perhaps broke the law.

The horse race on Main Street in Rapid City looks like a scene outside the O.K. Corral.

No doubt the pursuit of leisure has at times been a distraction from more pressing duties. But in its rightful place it has made life rich.

The fellowship of the team effort, the creativity of children at play and the power of perspiration all bear fruit in a healthy society.

Fishing at the falls in Sioux Falls, circa 1900. *Courtesy of Siouxland Heritage Museums*

Skinny dipping in the Firesteel Creek near Mitchell, circa 1890. Two of the boys are Sam and Al Weller. *Courtesy of Mitchell Area Historical Society*

C. Harman, F.A. Countryman, and others on Lake Kampeska near Watertown, circa 1895. *Courtesy of Codington County Heritage Museum and Historical Society*

Fred Korte family boating on the James River in Tacoma Park near Aberdeen, circa 1900. *Courtesy of Dacotah Prairie Museum*

Picnicking on Stony Point at Lake Kampeska near Watertown, 1907. *Courtesy of Codington County Heritage Museum and Historical Society*

Mitchell High School football team, 1907, won the South Dakota State Championship. Front row, left to right: captain Paul P. Sheeks, Edward Vassar, and Russell Jensen. Second row: Guy Cook, Albert "Nig" Nolt, Ray L. Blynn, Fred S. Porter, and O.B. "Berry" Wallace. Third row: Dr. K.E. Stair, Al Notson, coach R.E. Nichol, Ben Dickson, and Mark Storer. *Courtesy of Mitchell Area Historical Society*

Ice skating at Dakota Wesleyan University in Mitchell, circa 1910. *Courtesy of Mitchell Area Historical Society*

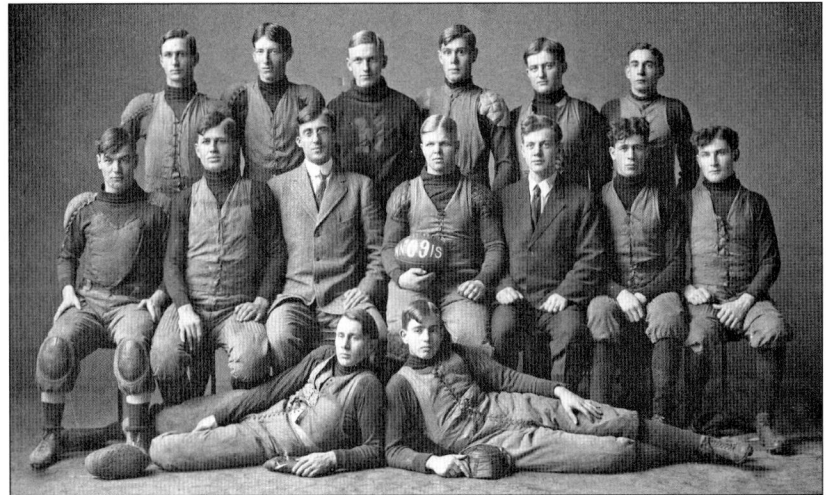

Northern Normal and Industrial School football team, 1908-09. *Courtesy of Dacotah Prairie Museum*

Watertown High School football team, 1906. *Courtesy of Codington County Heritage Museum and Historical Society*

A horse race on Main Street, Rapid City, circa 1910. *Courtesy of South Dakota State Historical Society*

Skating on Bartron Field on South Broadway, Watertown, circa 1915. *Courtesy of Codington County Heritage Museum and Historical Society*

The Mitchell Country Club, 1915. *Courtesy of Mitchell Area Historical Society*

Methodist church group from Pierre on the "Scotty Philip," circa 1915. *Courtesy of South Dakota State Historical Society*

The 1910 South Dakota State College baseball team. Back row, left to right: coach J.M. Saundson, Eugene Else, Elmer Anderson, and Ray Fridley. Center row: Fay Atkinson, Clarence Pier, Owen Hyde, George Brown, and William Sauder. Front row: Vern Wohlheter and Everett Dunn. *Courtesy of Brookings County History Museum*

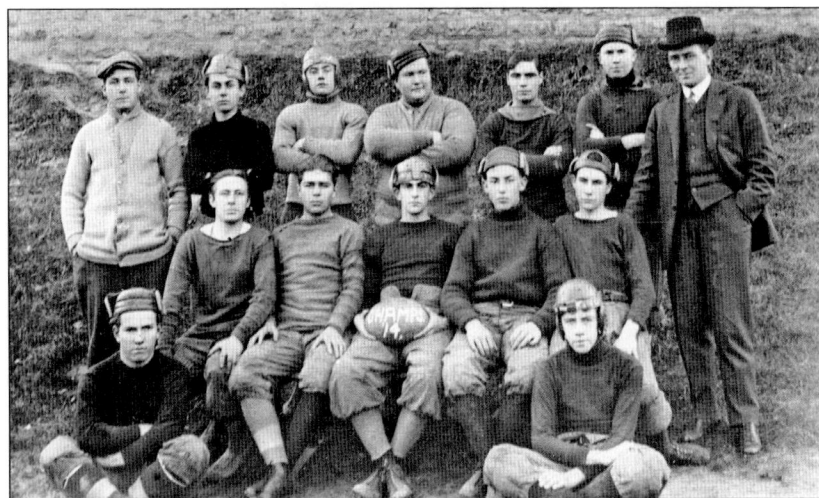

The 1914 Yankton championship football team. *Courtesy of Yankton County Historical Society*

Mitchell High School football team, 1917. In front, left to right: Perry Foss, Ed Parcells, Doyle Harmon, and Steve Coughlin. First row: Meredith Sweet, Fred Scallin, Coach Keskigo, captain Charles Barnard, Al Weller, and Loyde Johnson. Second row: Ralph Diehl, Elgie Coacher, Si Funston, L.W. Larson, and Mike Kinport. Back row: Ted Rowe, Ilo Sincox, George Holleran, Dick Smith, and Heyler Alexander. *Courtesy of Mitchell Area Historical Society*

Aberdeen Cubs baseball team. *Courtesy of Dacotah Prairie Museum*

Aberdeen High School District Champion basketball team, March 7, 1921. From left to right: Ben "Yid" Lazowsky, Justin "Mick" McCarthy, Dan "Percy" Drake, Merrit "Parrot" Hughes, Clarence "Dutch" Arendsee, Bill Welsh, Homer "Slitz" Stater, Frank "Bigada Foutz" Stablien, and coach D.A. "D.A.G." Glascock. *Courtesy of Dacotah Prairie Museum*

Brookings High School football team, 1926. Included are: Ray Schultz, Stanley Rishoi, Walter Matson, Edward Matson, Rolland McKnight, Solomon Kramer, James Wilson, Clyde Caldwell, Clark Trygstad, Loys Johnson, Raymond Johnson, Conrad Oyloe, Burton Simkins, Harry Steele, Emanuel Korstad, Boyd Bankert, Earl Spooner, Myron Ronning, Allen Farrankop, and coach Bob Coffey. *Courtesy of Brookings County History Museum*

Sports team from Columbus College, Sioux Falls, circa 1930. *Courtesy of Siouxland Heritage Museums*

Enjoying the water at the temporary municipal bathing beach, Lake Mitchell, 1928. *Courtesy of Mitchell Area Historical Society*

Williams Resort at Stony Point on Lake Kampeska near Watertown, circa 1930. *Courtesy of Codington County Heritage Museum and Historical Society*

Club house at the Mitchell Municipal Golf Course, circa 1932. *Courtesy of Mitchell Area Historical Society*

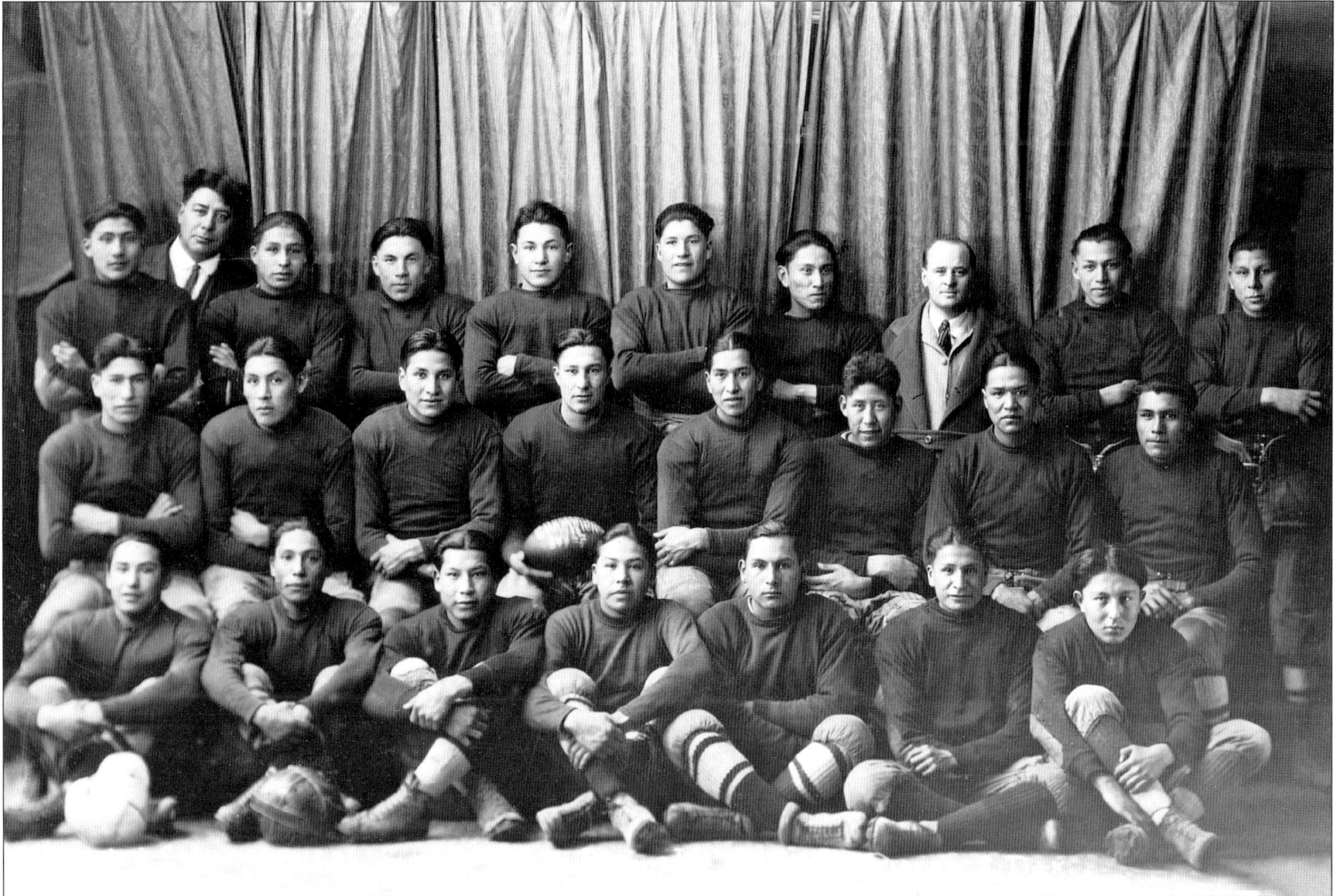

The Pierre Indian School undefeated football team of 1926. They outscored their opponents 349-7. *Courtesy of South Dakota State Historical Society*

Capital City Cowboys, a Pierre baseball team, June 28, 1929. *Courtesy of South Dakota State Historical Society*

Volga High School football team, 1932. They remained unbeaten for nine games. Front row, left to right: Herman Bortnes, Clarence Wood, Irvin Oines, Leonard Lee, Karl Kildahl, Stan Hammer, Rolf Stumley, and Vernon Erickson. Second row: Gerhard Nelson, Virgil VanMaanen, Roy Hanson, Rich Henry, Lyle Sundet, Martin Baker, Ray Kallemeyn, Dave Henry, and Donald Breed. Back row: Coach Myklebust, Donald Lee, Walter Leite, Everett Lee, Walter Leite, Everett Lee, Phil Haas, Louis Scanlan, Dan Wiersma, Leroy Oldenkamp, and Julius Piebenga. *Courtesy of Brookings County History Museum*

Celebrations & Events

South Dakotans have taken to heart the right to peaceably assemble.

They packed the street in front of the Corn Palace for Teddy Roosevelt Day. They stood in support when William Jennings Bryan came to explain his latest try for president. They listened to platitudes about patriotism and heard boasting at ground breakings. They considered the future whenever someone laid a cornerstone for a county courthouse. When veterans returned, cheers followed them from the train depot to main street. When a celebrity arrived to speak on a flag-draped platform, applause flowed as a matter of civic duty.

South Dakotans knew from the start that the way to celebrate democracy is by participating.

Service Day parade on Phillips Avenue, Sioux Falls, May 21, 1919. *Courtesy of Siouxland Heritage Museums*

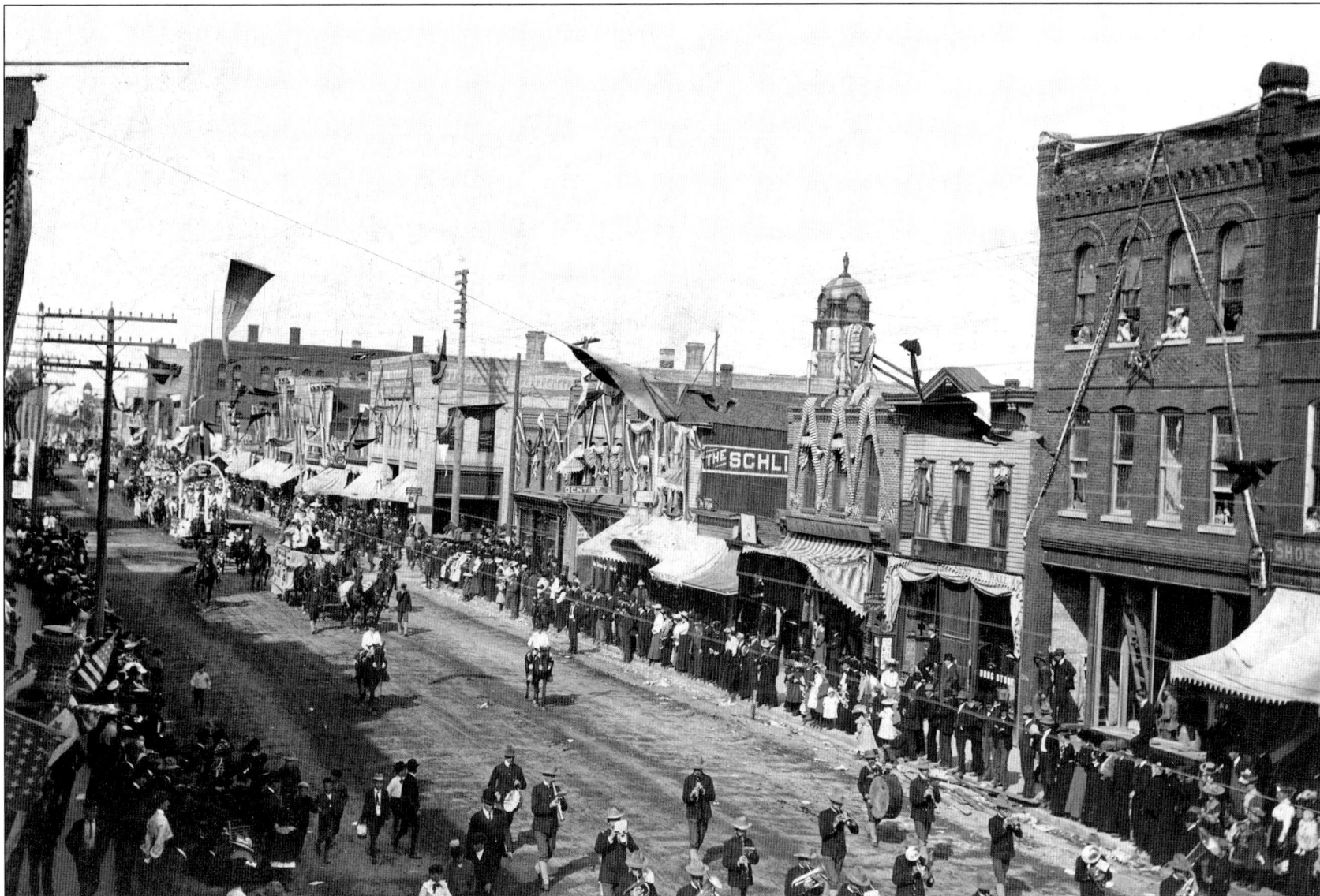

Carnival Day in Aberdeen, October 1, 1903. *Courtesy of Dacotah Prairie Museum*

Market Day Parade, Rapid City, July 24, 1909. *Courtesy of South Dakota State Historical Society*

Watertown Nursery float in a Watertown parade. *Courtesy of Codington County Heritage Museum and Historical Society*

Brookings Fourth of July parade, circa 1910. The Skinner building in the background was built in 1901; Brookings House, also pictured, burned in 1910. *Courtesy of Brookings County History Museum*

Roosevelt Day at Sioux Falls, September 3, 1910. *Courtesy of Siouxland Heritage Museums*

Homecoming parade in Yankton, June 1911. *Courtesy of Yankton County Historical Society*

Laying the cornerstone for the Brookings Courthouse, May 10, 1911. *Courtesy of Brookings County History Museum*

Laying of the cornerstone for the Yankton Elks Lodge, June 1912. *Courtesy of Yankton County Historical Society*

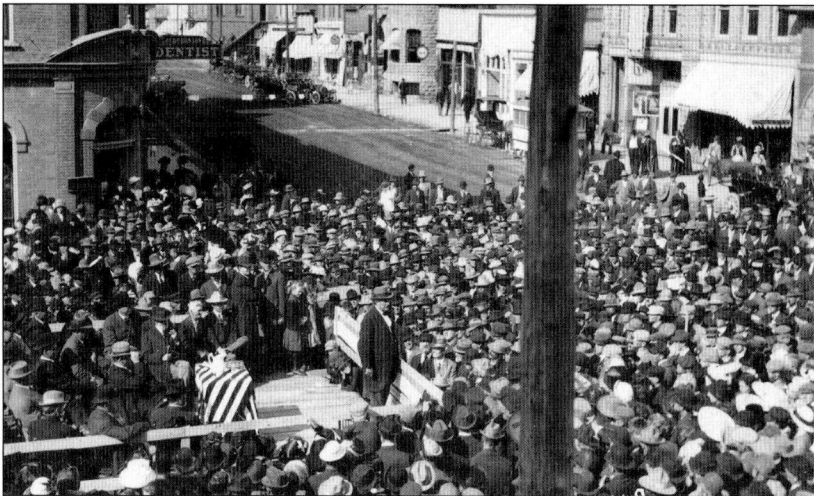

William Jennings Bryan campaigning in Yankton, October 7, 1912. *Courtesy of Yankton County Historical Society*

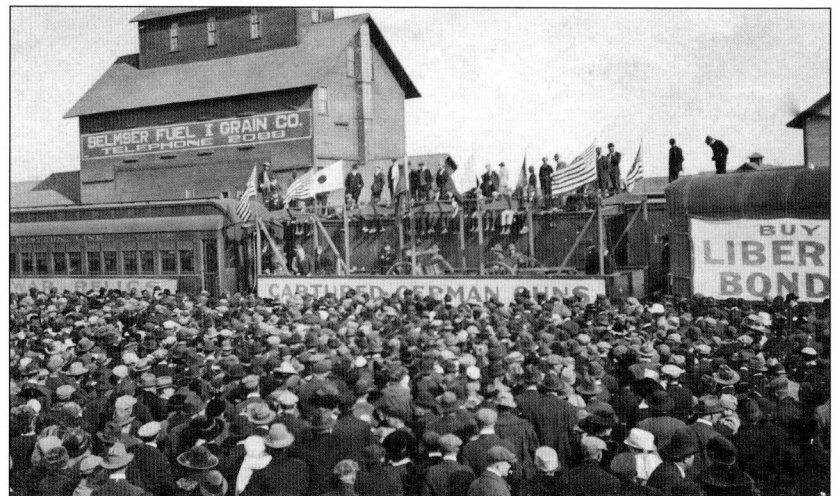

World War I troops returning, 1919. *Courtesy of Codington County Heritage Museum and Historical Society*

Service Day Parade in Sioux Falls, 1917. *Courtesy of Siouxland Heritage Museums*

A crowd gathered for Teddy Roosevelt Day at the Mitchell Corn Palace, 5th Avenue and Main Street, September 24, 1914. The Elks Lodge is on the right.

Courtesy of Mitchell Area Historical Society

Centennial Gateway Dedication at John Morrell Company, Sioux Falls, September 28, 1927. Plant Supt. H.F. Veenker is speaking. *Courtesy of Siouxland Heritage Museums*

Patriot's Day, Yankton, circa 1925. *Courtesy of Yankton County Historical Society*

Parade celebrating the end of World War I, Watertown, 1919. *Courtesy of Codington County Heritage Museum and Historical Society*

A 4-H rally at the C.B.H. during the Good Roads Fair in front of the Corn Palace in Mitchell, February 7, 1931. *Courtesy of Mitchell Area Historical Society*

Charles Lindbergh speaking at Renner Airfield, Sioux Falls, 1927. *Courtesy of Siouxland Heritage Museums*

Disasters

In a comparison of states, South Dakota has always been larger than average in area and much smaller than average in population.

There's a reason for that.

Floods and fires can happen about anywhere. But the wind, the snow, the cold and drought have a bleak peculiarity to them that speaks directly to South Dakota's image.

Hardship builds character, however, and the state and its communities always have moved forward, stronger for the experience.

Nobody cheered when the grasshoppers came, or the tornadoes, or the black blizzard of dust that brought nightfall to the middle of one afternoon in May.

Those who endured mourned their loss and then faced tomorrow.

Wind erosion scene in rural South Dakota, 1935. *Courtesy of Siouxland Heritage Museums*

Steamboats in the ice gorge at Yankton in the spring of 1881. *Courtesy of Yankton County Historical Society*

View of the west side of Main Street, Aberdeen, looking north from the Sherman House corner after the big blizzard of January 4, 1897. *Courtesy of Dacotah Prairie Museum*

Aberdeen flooded in 1897. *Courtesy of Dacotah Prairie Museum*

Train wreck at Elkton in Brookings County, 1904. *Courtesy of Brookings County History Museum*

Phillips Avenue, Sioux Falls, following a 1909 blizzard. *Courtesy of Siouxland Heritage Museums*

Fire at the Brookings House Hotel, Saturday morning, March 19, 1910.
Courtesy of Brookings County History Museum

Fire in Yankton on July 3, 1910. *Courtesy of Yankton County Historical Society*

Chicago, Milwaukee & St. Paul Railroad fire, January 23, 1911, in Aberdeen.
Courtesy of Dacotah Prairie Museum

Alexander Mitchell Hotel on fire, November 3, 1913, 6:30 a.m. The hotel was located at 3rd Avenue and Main Street. *Courtesy of Mitchell Area Historical Society*

Flood of the Missouri River at Pierre, August 29, 1912. *Courtesy of South Dakota State Historical Society*

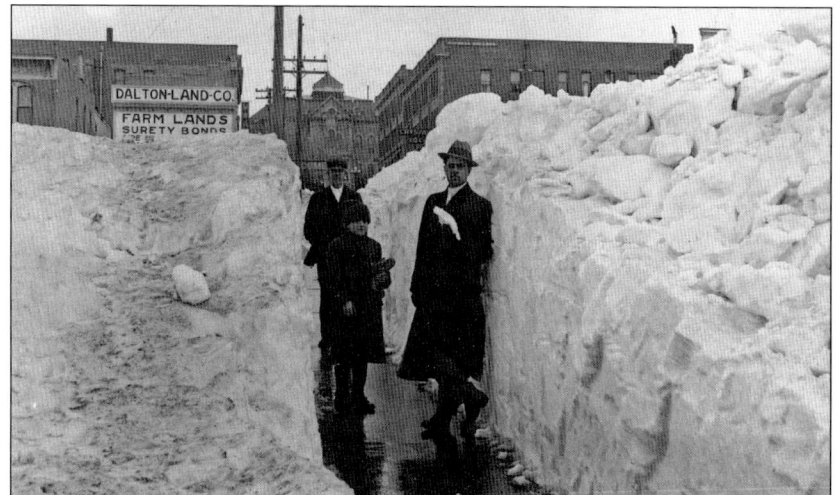

After a major snowfall in Pierre, 1913. *Courtesy of South Dakota State Historical Society*

A cyclone hit Watertown, 1914. *Courtesy of Codington County Heritage Museum and Historical Society*

After the Pennington County Bank fire, January 24, 1915. *Courtesy of South Dakota State Historical Society*

Fire at the Gale Theater in Mitchell on March 20, 1914. *Courtesy of Mitchell Area Historical Society*

Wreckage at the fairgrounds at Aberdeen, July 2, 1921. *Courtesy of Dacotah Prairie Museum*

The 1923 fire of Hentges-Smith Company in Watertown. *Courtesy of Codington County Heritage Museum and Historical Society*

Flood in Yankton, May 1926. *Courtesy of Yankton County Historical Society*

Crops destroyed by a grasshopper infestation in rural Sioux Falls, 1931.

Courtesy of Siouxland Heritage Museums

"Black Blizzard," May 9, 1934 at 3 p.m., as the dust blew in Watertown.

Courtesy of Dacotah Prairie Museum

Community

Every town that grew to a city had something to offer people. Some gave. Some received. Most did both. But nobody did neither.

Communities have always been about the human exchange, and where there are people the opportunity for exchange is great.

It's more than buying used cars and groceries. It's cooperating to push a just cause or to build a courthouse or to clean up after a tornado.

Groups unified around music and uniforms and slogans and customs. Some offered entertainment on a street corner, others salvation for the soul.

They all offered something irresistible, which was the occasion to rub shoulders, shake hands or look someone in the eye as a sign of trust and interdependence.

Communities wouldn't have it any other way.

Capital City Band, Pierre, circa 1910. *Courtesy of South Dakota State Historical Society*

First Masonic Temple in Aberdeen, July 23, 1897. *Courtesy of Dacotah Prairie Museum*

Old Settlers Association, Yankton. *Courtesy of Yankton County Historical Society*

State Juvenile Band, Mitchell, circa 1895. *Courtesy of Mitchell Area Historical Society*

Salvation Army band performing in Brookings. *Courtesy of Brookings County History Museum*

Baptist Church, Brookings, was organized in 1880. The church was built in 1882 at a cost of $3,000. *Courtesy of Brookings County History Museum*

Sacred Heart Church on the northwest corner of Fifth and Capitol streets, Yankton, was built in 1876. *Courtesy of Yankton County Historical Society*

Interior of First Immaculate Conception Church in southeast Watertown with the congregation's first permanently assigned priest, Father Peter Lauer. *Courtesy of Codington County Heritage Museum and Historical Society*

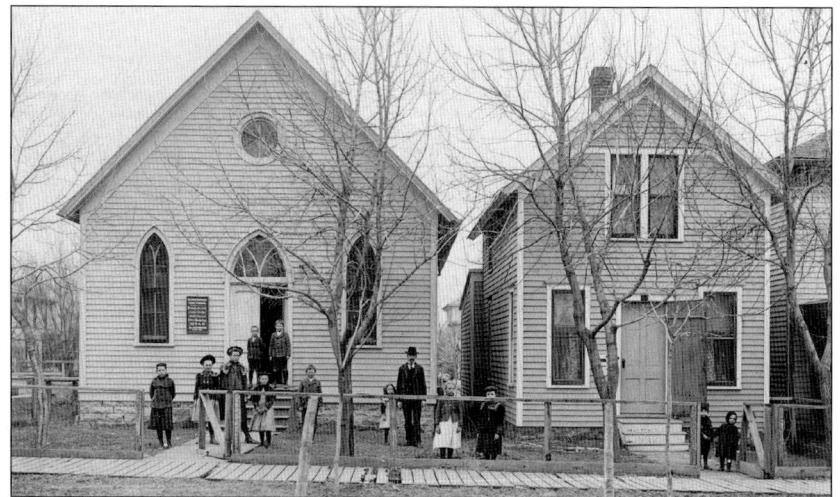

German Lutheran Zion Church and house, Sioux Falls, circa 1890. *Courtesy of Siouxland Heritage Museums*

Interior of the Aberdeen Grain Palace prior to 1897. *Courtesy of Dacotah Prairie Museum*

Emericks Opera Band, corner of Main and Seventh streets in Rapid City, 1908. The fountain in the middle of the street was for horses. *Courtesy of South Dakota State Historical Society*

Registering for Rosebud Lands at Yankton, July 18, 1904. The line ran from Second to Fourth streets. *Courtesy of Yankton County Historical Society*

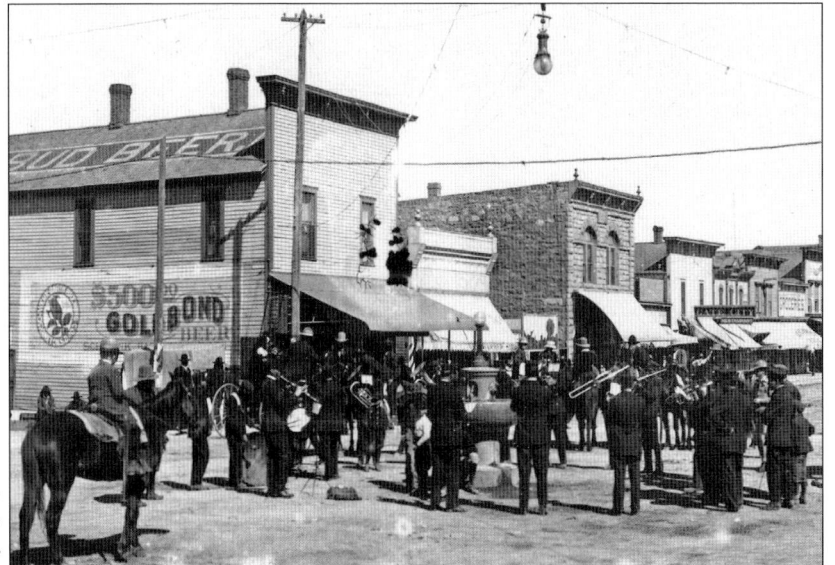

Pioneers of Dakota Territory. Front row, left to right: H.T. Bailey, first party of emigrants to Yankton; J.H. Shober, President of First Territorial Council; William Jayne, first Governor of Dakota Territory; and J.R. Hanson, chief clerk of First Territorial House. Back row: G.W. Kingsbury, editor of the first newspaper in Dakota, and J.C. Holman, builder of the first cabin in Yankton. *Courtesy of Yankton County Historical Society*

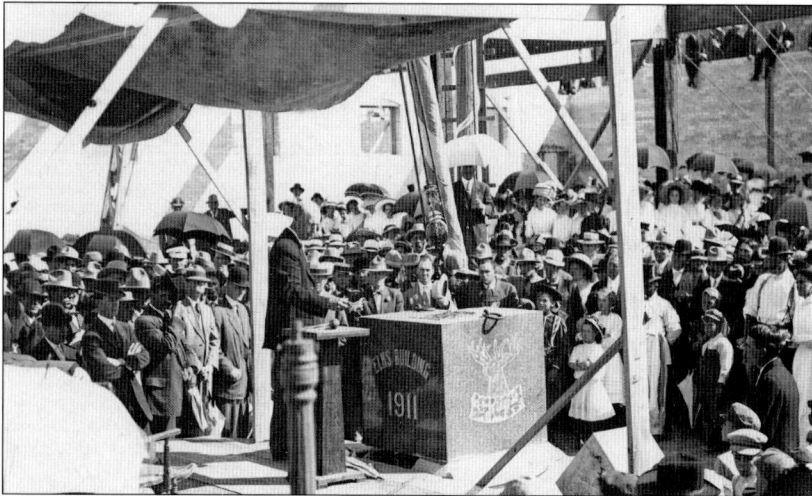

Laying the cornerstone for the Elks building, Rapid City, 1911. *Courtesy of South Dakota State Historical Society*

St. Joseph's Hospital, Mitchell. *Courtesy of Mitchell Area Historical Society*

Chorus for the Honeywell revival meetings which were held in Aberdeen January 1 through February 6, 1915, on the corner of Seventh Avenue and Main Street South. *Courtesy of Dacotah Prairie Museum*

Alfalfa Palace, Rapid City, 1917. *Courtesy of South Dakota State Historical Society*

Methodist State Hospital, Mitchell. *Courtesy of Mitchell Area Historical Society*

Sioux Falls Drum Corps, circa 1920. *Courtesy of Siouxland Heritage Museums*

First Lutheran Church confirmation class, Brookings, circa 1923. B.A. Benson was the pastor from 1915 to 1936. *Courtesy of Brookings County History Museum*

The Fourth Infantry Band on the steps of Carnegie Library in Watertown.

Courtesy of Codington County Heritage Museum and Historical Society

Aberdeen Municipal Band, 1922. *Courtesy of Dacotah Prairie Museum*

Performing on WNAX Radio in Yankton is the orchestra voted No. 1 in the United States by Radio Digest magazine, 1928. From left to right: Joe Salvatore, conductor Art Harbing, Zeke Stout, Joe Fejfar, Frank Hobbs, Bob Blacker, Charles Stinback, Joe Jarolim, Corrine Horst, Harvy Nelson, Randy Christensen, and John Matuska. *Courtesy of Yankton County Historical Society*

Standing outside the First Congregational Church after their final service in that building, Pierre, July 10, 1932. *Courtesy of South Dakota State Historical Society*

Mitchell Kiwanis Good Fellows distributing clothing and toys for Christmas, 1928, Mitchell. Kiwanians, left to right: Art Bjodstrup; John H. Giese, who owned the truck; George Phifer; John J. Klundt; Carl Ralston; and Robert Raines. The truck is standing in front of the west side of the Widmann Hotel on South Main Street. *Courtesy of Mitchell Area Historical Society*

Volga Lutheran Church Aid in front of East Church, November 1930. Rev. Kildahl is in the center of the second row. *Courtesy of Brookings County History Museum*

Dedication and laying the cornerstone for St. Mary's Hospital, Pierre, May 18, 1930. *Courtesy of South Dakota State Historical Society*

Members of the American Legion Post #8 of Pierre, October 1930. Commander O'Neil was representing the National Organization and Carroll Lockhart the Department of South Dakota. The Onida Drum and Bugle Corps is to the right. *Courtesy of South Dakota State Historical Society*

Banton Amphitheater in Foerster's Park (aka Forester's Park), Yankton, circa 1927. *Courtesy of Yankton County Historical Society*

First Avenue Northwest in Watertown during the Threshermen's Picnic, circa 1936. *Courtesy of Codington County Heritage Museum and Historical Society*

Gathered at the depot for the "Days of '81" celebration in Pierre, 1930. *Courtesy of South Dakota State Historical Society*